What Child Is This?

by Martha Marshall
illustrated by
James Conaway

Published by The Dandelion House
A Division of The Child's World

Distributed by Scripture Press Publications, Wheaton, Illinois 60187.

Library of Congress Cataloging in Publication Data

Marshall, Martha.
  What child is this?

  Summary: Simple text and illustrations retell the
birth of Jesus.
  1. Jesus Christ—Nativity—Juvenile literature.
[1. Jesus Christ—Nativity] I. Conaway, James, 1944-
ill. ` II. Title.
BT315.2.027   232.9'2   82-7239
ISBN 0-89693-204-4   AACR2

Published by The Dandelion House, A Division of The Child's World, Inc.
© 1982 SP Publications, Inc. All rights reserved. Printed in U.S.A.

1 2 3 4 5 6 7 8 9 10 11 12 R 89 88 87 86 85 84 83 82

What Child Is This?

In Bethlehem one starry night,

a baby boy was born—
born in a stable
and laid in a manger.

Most of the people in Bethlehem
did not know who the child was.
But Mary, His mother, knew!
An angel had told her.
Mary knew that her baby boy
was Jesus, God's own Son.
And Mary loved Him.

Joseph, Mary's husband, knew!
An angel had told him.
Joseph knew that Mary's baby boy
was Jesus, God's own Son.
And Joseph loved and cared for Him.

Most of the people in Bethlehem
did not know who the child was.
But the shepherds knew!
An angel told them of Jesus' birth,
and the shepherds hurried
to Bethlehem.

They searched until they found
the baby, lying in a manger.
They knew this tiny child
was Jesus, God's own Son.
And they told others about Him.

Mary and Joseph took the baby
to God's house, the temple.
Most of the people in the temple
did not know who the child was.
But Simeon knew!
Simeon was an old, old man
who had been waiting to see God's Son.
Simeon knew that this baby boy
was the one he had waited for.
And Simeon thanked God for Him.

Someone else in the temple knew!
Anna knew.
Anna was an old, old woman
who lived in the temple.
Anna knew that the tiny baby
was Jesus, God's own Son.
She, too, thanked God for Him.

Most of the people in the world
did not know who the child was.
But the wise men knew!
In a faraway land, they saw a star.
They traveled miles and miles
to find the baby king.

The wise men knew that the child
was Jesus, God's own Son.
And they brought gifts
and worshipped Him.

Still today, many, many people
do not know who the child was.
But we know!
We know that the child of Bethlehem
was Jesus, God's own Son.

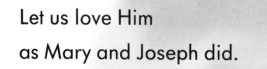

Let us love Him
as Mary and Joseph did.

Let us tell others about Him
as the shepherds did.

Let us thank God for Him
as Simeon and Anna did.

Let us worship Him
as the wise men
did.

What child is this?

This child is Jesus, God's own Son.